PRAYING *the* BIBLE INTO YOUR LIFE

STORMIE OMARTIAN

HARVEST HOUSE PUBLISHERS

EUGENE, OREGON

Cover by Koechel Peterson & Associates, Inc., Minneapolis, Minnesota

Cover photo © iStockphoto / Thinkstock

Back cover author photo © Michael Gomez Photography

PRAYING THE BIBLE INTO YOUR LIFE

Copyright © 2012 by Stormie Omartian
Published by Harvest House Publishers
Eugene, Oregon 97402
www.harvesthousepublishers.com

ISBN 978-0-7369-4773-2 (pbk.)
ISBN 978-0-7369-4774-9 (eBook)

Printed in the United States of America

12 13 14 15 16 17 18 19 20 / BP-SK / 10 9 8 7 6 5 4 3 2 1

*Your word I have hidden
in my heart, that I might
not sin against You.*
PSALM 119:11

This book is dedicated to Kim Moore,
who is not only my wonderful editor at Harvest House,
but also a precious and priceless friend,
encourager, and fellow animal lover
who believes—as I do—that dogs and cats
are on the list of God's gifts of love to us.

Thank you, Kim, for all your tireless work
for me and the Lord.

Introduction

We cannot live successfully without God's Word in our heart. We must not only read it, but we must also hear it, speak it, remember it, and ask God to weave it into our soul so that it changes us and becomes part of the fabric of our lives. One of the best ways to see that happen is to include Scriptures in your prayers.

In this book I have taken Scriptures from every part of the Bible in order to illustrate how to include a verse into your prayers so that it inspires you to pray as the Holy Spirit leads you. I believe that by the time you finish this book you will be praying the Bible into your life every time you read it. And you will love God's Word even more each time you do.

- Stormie Omartian

You Are God's Creation

God created man in His own image;
in the image of God He created him;
male and female He created them.

GENESIS 1:27

Lord, I thank You for the beauty and wonder of Your awesome creation. Thank You for creating me. I pray that more and more of Your likeness would be revealed in me as I walk each day with You.

God Keeps His Promises to You

I set My rainbow in the cloud,
and it shall be for the sign of the
covenant between Me and the earth.

GENESIS 9:13

Lord, I praise You for Your absolute faithfulness to Your promises. No matter what circumstances threaten to overwhelm me, I know I can trust in You to sustain me.

Trust God's Plan for Your Life

Do not therefore be grieved or angry with yourselves because you sold me here; for God sent me before you to preserve life.

GENESIS 45:5

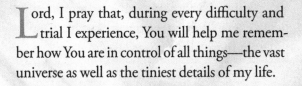

Lord, I pray that, during every difficulty and trial I experience, You will help me remember how You are in control of all things—the vast universe as well as the tiniest details of my life.

God Saves You in Many Ways

Do not be afraid. Stand still, and
see the salvation of the LORD, which
He will accomplish for you today.

EXODUS 14:13

Lord, I praise You for Your great salvation. Thank You for taking all fear from me and giving me a heart full of thanks for the wonderful ways in which You have saved me.

God Makes Himself Known to You

The LORD said to Moses, "Go to the people and consecrate them today and tomorrow, and let them wash their clothes. And let them be ready for the third day. For on the third day the LORD will come down upon Mount Sinai in the sight of all the people."

EXODUS 19:10-11

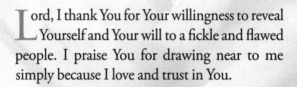

Lord, I thank You for Your willingness to reveal Yourself and Your will to a fickle and flawed people. I praise You for drawing near to me simply because I love and trust in You.

God Helps You to Understand His Ways

*Show me now Your way, that
I may know You and that I may
find grace in Your sight.*

Exodus 33:13

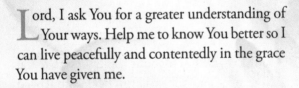

Lord, I ask You for a greater understanding of Your ways. Help me to know You better so I can live peacefully and contentedly in the grace You have given me.

Be Grateful for
What Jesus Did

*Offer the offering of the people,
and make atonement for them,
as the LORD commanded.*

LEVITICUS 9:7

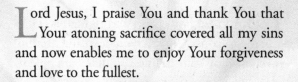

Lord Jesus, I praise You and thank You that Your atoning sacrifice covered all my sins and now enables me to enjoy Your forgiveness and love to the fullest.

Honor the Lord for His Holiness

*This is what the LORD spoke, saying:
"By those who come near Me I must
be regarded as holy; and before all
the people I must be glorified."*

LEVITICUS 10:3

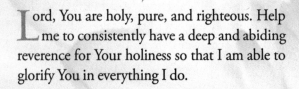

Lord, You are holy, pure, and righteous. Help me to consistently have a deep and abiding reverence for Your holiness so that I am able to glorify You in everything I do.

Ask God to Help You Live a Holy Life

You shall be holy, for I the LORD your God am holy.

LEVITICUS 19:2

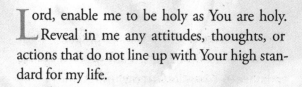

Lord, enable me to be holy as You are holy. Reveal in me any attitudes, thoughts, or actions that do not line up with Your high standard for my life.

Bask in the Light of the Lord

The LORD bless you and keep you;
the LORD make His face shine
upon you, and be gracious to you;
the LORD lift up His countenance
upon you, and give you peace.

NUMBERS 6:24-26

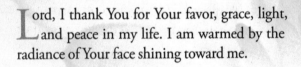

Lord, I thank You for Your favor, grace, light, and peace in my life. I am warmed by the radiance of Your face shining toward me.

Show Appreciation for God's Blessings to You

*When the people complained,
it displeased the LORD.*

NUMBERS 11:1

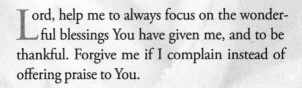

Lord, help me to always focus on the wonderful blessings You have given me, and to be thankful. Forgive me if I complain instead of offering praise to You.

Pray for Others to Be Free of Sin

Pardon the iniquity of this people, I pray, according to the greatness of Your mercy.

NUMBERS 14:19

Lord, I bring before You my brothers and sisters in Christ and ask that You would forgive their sins and intervene in their lives with Your love and mercy. Teach me to pray in power for others.

Love God with Your Whole Heart

You shall love the LORD your God with all your heart, with all your soul, and with all your strength.

DEUTERONOMY 6:5

Lord, help me to love You with everything that is within me. Thank You for Your unfailing love for me. Forgive me when I don't reflect Your love by loving others the way that You do.

Refuse to Neglect God's Word

Man shall not live by bread alone;
but man lives by every word that
proceeds from the mouth of the LORD.

DEUTERONOMY 8:3

Lord, help me to make reading Your Word a priority every day. I know I cannot live successfully without it. Forgive me when I am careless about this.

Consider the Consequences

All these blessings shall come upon
you and overtake you, because you
obey the voice of the LORD your God.

DEUTERONOMY 28:2

Lord, help me to obey You so that my life is
open to Your many blessings. Keep me from
my own way so that I can always make right
choices. Teach me to follow Your leading.

God Is Always with You

As I was with Moses, so I will
be with you. I will not leave
you nor forsake you.

JOSHUA 1:5

Lord, I thank You for Your presence with me at all times. I take comfort in knowing You will never abandon me. Help me to remember that You continuously watch over me.

Be Separate from Uncleanness

Joshua said to the people, "Sanctify yourselves, for tomorrow the LORD will do wonders among you."

JOSHUA 3:5

⤜

Lord, I pray You will help me to separate myself from anything that is unclean in Your sight so that I can be devoted entirely to serving You and watching You do wondrous things in my life.

God Honors His Word to You

The Lord has kept me
alive, as He said.

Joshua 14:10

～

Lord, I praise You for Your faithfulness to always keep Your Word and sustain me. Help me to have that same kind of faithfulness to keep my word to You. Give me the ability to trust Your Word no matter what is happening in my life.

You Can Be a Light to Others

Let those who love Him be
like the sun when it comes
out in full strength.

JUDGES 5:31

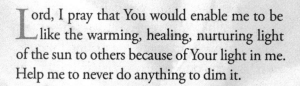

Lord, I pray that You would enable me to be like the warming, healing, nurturing light of the sun to others because of Your light in me. Help me to never do anything to dim it.

Worship Only God

*They put away the foreign gods from
among them and served the LORD.*

JUDGES 10:16

Lord, help me to put away all idols and false
gods. Show me where I have allowed anything into my heart that is not of You. I want to
serve You and only You.

God Can Do Anything

*The Angel of the L{\small ORD} appeared
to the woman and said to her,
"Indeed now, you are barren and
have borne no children, but you
shall conceive and bear a son."*

J{\small UDGES} 13:3

Lord, I thank You that You can do anything.
You can even birth something in my life
where there seemed to be no hope of it now.
Give me great faith to believe for the wonderful
things You want to do in me.

God Is Your Refuge

*The LORD repay your work, and
a full reward be given you by the
LORD God of Israel, under whose
wings you have come for refuge.*

RUTH 2:12

❧

Lord, help me to fully learn what it means to
take refuge in You. I want to stay close to
You at all times and not be tempted away. Thank
You for the great reward You give to those who
seek You.

Listen for God's Voice

Speak, LORD, for Your servant hears.
1 SAMUEL 3:9

❧

Lord, help me to clearly hear Your voice speaking to my heart. Enable me to silence the voices of distraction within me and around me so that I can better recognize Your instructions to my soul.

Keep Praying for Other People

*Moreover, as for me, far be it from
me that I should sin against the
LORD in ceasing to pray for you.*

1 Samuel 12:23

∾

Lord, help me to be a strong person of prayer for other people—especially for those whom You put on my heart or in my life. Show me ways to pray for them that I wouldn't know to do otherwise.

Refuse to Rebel Against God

*Rebellion is as the sin of
witchcraft, and stubbornness
is as iniquity and idolatry.*

1 Samuel 15:23

⁓

Lord, I pray that I will not allow my own selfish desires to draw me away from living Your way. Help me to never be in opposition to Your law or leading.

God Looks on Your Heart

*The LORD said to Samuel, "Do not
look at his appearance or at his
physical stature, because I have
refused him. For the LORD does
not see as man sees; for man looks
at the outward appearance, but
the LORD looks at the heart."*

1 SAMUEL 16:7

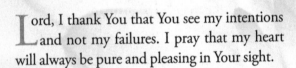

Lord, I thank You that You see my intentions
and not my failures. I pray that my heart
will always be pure and pleasing in Your sight.

Be Wise and Secure God's Favor

*David behaved wisely in all his
ways, and the LORD was with him.*

1 Samuel 18:14

❧

Lord, help me to have wisdom so I can behave
wisely in everything I do. I don't want to do
anything that would undermine the power of
Your presence in my life.

You Can Discern God's Will

*David inquired of the LORD, saying,
"Shall I go up against the Philistines?
Will You deliver them into my
hand?" And the LORD said to David,
"Go up, for I will doubtless deliver
the Philistines into your hand."*

2 SAMUEL 5:19

❧

Lord, I pray that You would give me an ever-increasing ability to discern Your will for my life. Help me to daily remember to ask You for wisdom and direction, and to thank You for providing me with the answers I seek.

Stop to Worship Often

*So it was, when those bearing the ark
of the LORD had gone six paces, that
he sacrificed oxen and fatted sheep.*

2 SAMUEL 6:13

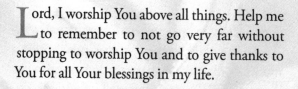

Lord, I worship You above all things. Help me
to remember to not go very far without
stopping to worship You and to give thanks to
You for all Your blessings in my life.

Come Humbly to God and Confess Your Sins

David said to Nathan, "I have sinned against the Lord." And Nathan said to David, "The Lord also has put away your sin; you shall not die."

2 Samuel 12:13

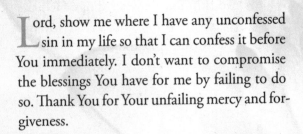

Lord, show me where I have any unconfessed sin in my life so that I can confess it before You immediately. I don't want to compromise the blessings You have for me by failing to do so. Thank You for Your unfailing mercy and forgiveness.

Ask God for Wisdom

Give to Your servant an
understanding heart.

1 KINGS 3:9

～

Lord, I ask You for wisdom, just as King Solomon did, so that I might live in ways that honor and please You. I know that the wisdom You give to me will bring a long and good life. I also know it begins with a deep love and reverence for You.

Turn Your Heart
to Devotion for God

*His wives turned his heart after
other gods; and his heart was
not loyal to the LORD his God.*

1 KINGS 11:4

Lord, I ask that You would reveal to me any desires, thoughts, possessions, diversions, or relationships in my life that are more important to me than my devotion to You. Help me to choose You first above all else so that my heart remains unfailingly loyal to You.

Listen for God's Still Small Voice

*The LORD passed by, and a great and strong
wind tore into the mountains and broke
the rocks in pieces before the LORD, but
the LORD was not in the wind; and after
the wind an earthquake, but the LORD
was not in the earthquake; and after the
earthquake a fire, but the LORD was not in
the fire; and after the fire a still small voice.*

1 KINGS 9:11-12

Lord, I thank You that You speak to my heart.
Help me to silence and crowd out the noise
and distraction of the world around me so that I
can clearly hear Your gentle voice.

Don't Keep Quiet When You Have Good News

They said to one another, "We are not doing right. This day is a day of good news, and we remain silent."

2 Kings 7:9

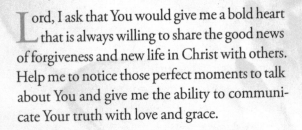

Lord, I ask that You would give me a bold heart that is always willing to share the good news of forgiveness and new life in Christ with others. Help me to notice those perfect moments to talk about You and give me the ability to communicate Your truth with love and grace.

Hold Fast to God

*He held fast to the LORD; he did
not depart from following Him,
but kept His commandments.*

2 KINGS 18:6

Lord, I want to cling to You every moment with
my whole heart. Help me to never stray from
Your commandments. Enable me to always live
Your way.

Pray for Righteous Leaders

He did what was right in the sight of the L<small>ORD</small>, and walked in all the ways of his father David; he did not turn aside to the right hand or to the left.

2 K<small>INGS</small> 22:2

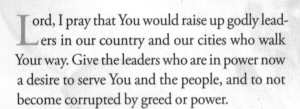

Lord, I pray that You would raise up godly leaders in our country and our cities who walk Your way. Give the leaders who are in power now a desire to serve You and the people, and to not become corrupted by greed or power.

Ask God to Bless You

Jabez called on the God of Israel saying, "Oh, that You would bless me indeed, and enlarge my territory, that Your hand would be with me, and that You would keep me from evil, that I may not cause pain!"

1 CHRONICLES 4:10

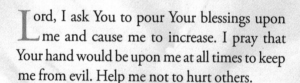

Lord, I ask You to pour Your blessings upon me and cause me to increase. I pray that Your hand would be upon me at all times to keep me from evil. Help me not to hurt others.

God Will Go Before You

*It shall be, when you hear a sound of
marching in the tops of the mulberry
trees, then you shall go out to battle,
for God has gone out before you to
strike the camp of the Philistines.*

1 CHRONICLES 14:15

Lord, I thank You that whenever I must face
my enemy, You will go before me to defeat
anything that opposes me.

Praise God Daily for His Salvation

Sing to the Lord, all the earth;
proclaim the good news of His
salvation from day to day.

1 Chronicles 16:23

❧

Lord, I thank You and praise You for saving me in every way I can be saved. Each day I wake up to the good news that I will spend my life and eternity with You.

Trust That with God, Nothing Is Impossible

Asa cried out to the LORD his God, and said, "LORD, it is nothing for You to help, whether with many or with those who have no power; help us, O LORD our God, for we rest on You, and in Your name we go against this multitude."

2 CHRONICLES 14:11

Lord, I bring to You my impossible situations and trust in Your infinite power to help me. I give up my worry and concerns and choose to rest confidently in You. Thank You that I can trust in the absolute authority of Your name.

If You Seek Him, You Will Find Him

The LORD is with you while you are with Him. If you seek Him, He will be found by you.

2 CHRONICLES 15:2

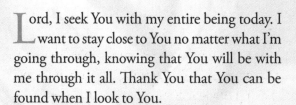

Lord, I seek You with my entire being today. I want to stay close to You no matter what I'm going through, knowing that You will be with me through it all. Thank You that You can be found when I look to You.

God Will Rescue You from Trouble

When he was in affliction, he implored the LORD his God, and humbled himself greatly before the God of his fathers, and prayed to Him; and He received his entreaty, heard his supplication, and brought him back to Jerusalem into his kingdom. Then Manasseh knew that the LORD was God.

2 CHRONICLES 33:12-13

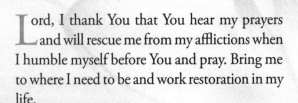

Lord, I thank You that You hear my prayers and will rescue me from my afflictions when I humble myself before You and pray. Bring me to where I need to be and work restoration in my life.

Ask God for a Generous Heart

According to their ability, they
gave to the treasury for the work.

EZRA 2:69

❧

Lord, please make me to be a generous person. I want to always be willing to give back to Your work. Help me remember that I am only a steward of all You have given me.

Never Neglect God's House

*All the people shouted with a
great shout, when they praised the
LORD, because the foundation of
the house of the LORD was laid.*

EZRA 3:11

Lord, help me to never neglect Your house, my place of worship. I praise You for the place You have given me where I can join with others to worship You. Enable me to give generously to help supply the needs there.

God Delivers You

The hand of our God was upon us, and He delivered us from the hand of the enemy and from ambush along the road.

EZRA 8:31

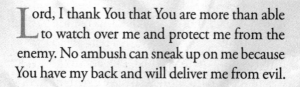

Lord, I thank You that You are more than able to watch over me and protect me from the enemy. No ambush can sneak up on me because You have my back and will deliver me from evil.

Be Ready for Battle

*Those who built on the wall, and
those who carried burdens, loaded
themselves so that with one hand
they worked at construction, and
with the other held a weapon.*

NEHEMIAH 4:17

Lord, I pray that You will equip me for battle
with weapons of warfare. Help me to know
how to use them against the enemy's attack
whenever I do the work You have given me to do.

Don't Be Intimidated by Fear

*They all were trying to make us
afraid, saying, "Their hands will
be weakened in the work, and it
will not be done." Now therefore,
O God, strengthen my hands.*

NEHEMIAH 6:9

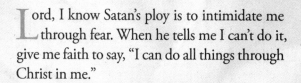

Lord, I know Satan's ploy is to intimidate me
through fear. When he tells me I can't do it,
give me faith to say, "I can do all things through
Christ in me."

Receive the Joy of the Lord

The joy of the LORD is your strength.
NEHEMIAH 8:10

❧

Lord, I pray that Your joy would rise in my heart this day and give me the gladness and strength I need to face the obstacles of life. Thank You that when I am weak, You are strong.

Find Favor with the King

The king loved Esther more than
all the other women, and she
obtained grace and favor in his sight
more than all the other virgins.

ESTHER 2:17

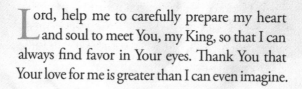

Lord, help me to carefully prepare my heart and soul to meet You, my King, so that I can always find favor in Your eyes. Thank You that Your love for me is greater than I can even imagine.

Be Aware of Your Calling

*Who knows whether you
have come to the kingdom
for such a time as this?*

ESTHER 4:14

⚬

Lord, no matter how afraid I am, I pray that
You would always give me the courage to do
what is right. Help me to hear Your voice leading
me to fulfill what You are calling me to do.

Tell What God Has Done

*These days should be remembered
and kept throughout every
generation…that the memory
of them should not perish
among their descendants.*

ESTHER 9:28

Lord, help me to speak to others about all You
have done in my life so that it is passed on
from one generation to another. Keep me from
being hesitant to tell others the good news about
You.

Praise God at All Times

*The LORD gave, and the LORD
has taken away; blessed be
the name of the LORD.*

JOB 1:21

~

Lord, please give me the kind of faith-filled
trust that enjoys Your blessings but does not
demand them or complain when they are with-
drawn. Help me to praise You at all times, no
matter what is happening.

Trust Your Redeemer

*I know that my Redeemer lives, and
He shall stand at last on the earth.*

Job 19:25

~

Lord, I thank You that You are my Redeemer
and You redeem all things. Thank You for
working redemption in my life in every situation.

Pray for God's Restoration

The LORD restored Job's losses
when he prayed for his friends.
Indeed the LORD gave Job twice
as much as he had before.

JOB 42:10

⌒

Lord, I thank You that Your redemption is far reaching. Help me to pray through every difficult situation so that You can bring the kind of restoration that causes life to be even better than it was before.

Live in God's Presence

LORD, who may abide in Your tabernacle? Who may dwell in Your holy hill? He who walks uprightly, and works righteousness, and speaks the truth in his heart.

PSALM 15:1-2

Lord, help me to walk in Your ways and obey Your commands. Help me be a person in whom the truth abides so that I will always speak what's right in every situation.

Let God Satisfy Your Soul

O God, You are my God; early will
I seek You; my soul thirsts for You;
my flesh longs for You in a dry and
thirsty land where there is no water.

PSALM 63:1

⁓

Lord, long for more of You. Only Your endless rivers of living water can satisfy my thirsty soul. Help me to seek the refreshment of Your presence first thing every day.

God Will Help
You Live His Way

*Give me understanding, and I shall
keep Your law; indeed, I shall
observe it with my whole heart.*

PSALM 119:34

❧

Lord, I ask that You would give me a deep
understanding of Your Word and help me
to obey it. Teach me Your truth so that I can
stand strong and pure in this generation.

Decide to Trust in the Lord

*Trust in the L*ORD *with all your*
heart, and lean not on your
own understanding; in all your
ways acknowledge Him, and
He shall direct your paths.

PROVERBS 3:5-6

Lord, help me to trust You more than I trust myself. Help me to acknowledge You in everything I do and not think I have it all figured out. I need You to give me guidance and keep me on the right path.

Treasure God's Commands

My son, keep my words, and
treasure my commands within
you. Keep my commands and live.

Proverbs 7:1-2

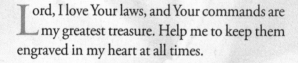

Lord, I love Your laws, and Your commands are my greatest treasure. Help me to keep them engraved in my heart at all times.

Seek Out Godly Friends

The righteous should choose his friends carefully, for the way of the wicked leads them astray.

PROVERBS 12:26

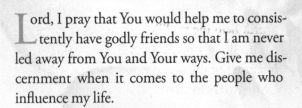

Lord, I pray that You would help me to consistently have godly friends so that I am never led away from You and Your ways. Give me discernment when it comes to the people who influence my life.

Give to Those in Need

He who gives to the poor will
not lack, but he who hides his
eyes will have many curses.

PROVERBS 28:27

Lord, help me to diligently be mindful of the
needs of others. I don't ever want to be
deserving of the consequences that come from
turning away from the poor and needy.

Know When It Is
Time to Let Go

To everything there is a season, a
time for every purpose under
heaven…a time to keep and
a time to throw away.

ECCLESIASTES 3:1,6

Lord, help me to see the things and people in
my life that I need to let go of and enable me
to do it. Show me all that I must keep safe and
hold close to my heart, and all that I must cast
aside.

Remember Who God Made You to Be

Dead flies putrefy the perfumer's ointment, and cause it to give off a foul odor; so does a little folly to one respected for wisdom and honor.

ECCLESIASTES 10:1

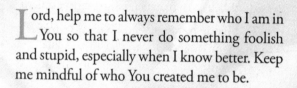

Lord, help me to always remember who I am in You so that I never do something foolish and stupid, especially when I know better. Keep me mindful of who You created me to be.

God Covers You with Love

*He brought me to the
banqueting house, and his
banner over me was love.*

SONG OF SOLOMON 2:4

⁓

Lord, I thank You that You prepare a feast before
me of all the good blessings You have for
my life. Thank You that Your love is an umbrella
over me, bringing protection and security.

Nothing Diminishes God's Love for You

Many waters cannot quench love,
nor can the floods drown it.

SONG OF SOLOMON 8:7

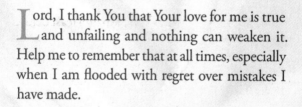

Lord, I thank You that Your love for me is true and unfailing and nothing can weaken it. Help me to remember that at all times, especially when I am flooded with regret over mistakes I have made.

God Cleanses You from All Sin

*"Come now, and let us reason together," says the L*ORD*, "though your sins are like scarlet, they shall be as white as snow."*

Isaiah 1:18

❧

Lord, how grateful I am to You that Your forgiveness is so complete that I am purified from all my sin and appear to You as white as new snow.

God Helps You
Know Good from Evil

Woe to those who call evil good,
and good evil; who put darkness
for light, and light for darkness.

❧

Lord, help me to always be able to clearly distinguish good from evil so that I don't fall into the confusion that is in the world today where people call good evil and darkness light.

Be Willing to Go Where God Leads

I heard the voice of the Lord,
saying: "Whom shall I send,
and who will go for Us?" Then
I said, "Here am I! Send me."

ISAIAH 6:8

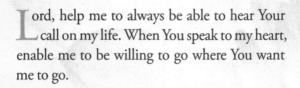

Lord, help me to always be able to hear Your call on my life. When You speak to my heart, enable me to be willing to go where You want me to go.

God Will Give You Strength

Those who wait on the LORD shall
renew their strength; they shall
mount up with wings like eagles.

ISAIAH 40:31

Lord, I wait on You with thanks for Your great-ness that allows me to "run and not be weary...walk and not faint" (Isaiah 40:31). Thank You for Your mercy and power that lifts me up when I'm weak and feel I can't go on.

Desire to Know God Better

Let him who glories glory in this,
that he understands and knows Me.

JEREMIAH 9:24

Lord, help me to never forget for even a moment that the greatest thing in my life is to know You, and to understand more each day about all of who You are.

Don't Hide from God

"Am I a God near at hand," says the
LORD, *"and not a God afar off? Can*
anyone hide himself in secret places,
so I shall not see him?" says the LORD.

JEREMIAH 23:23

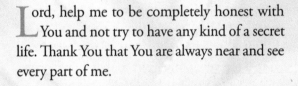

Lord, help me to be completely honest with
You and not try to have any kind of a secret
life. Thank You that You are always near and see
every part of me.

Keep God's Law
in Your Heart

*I will put My law in their
minds, and write it on their
hearts; and I will be their God,
and they shall be My people.*

JEREMIAH 31:33

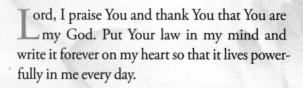

L ord, I praise You and thank You that You are
my God. Put Your law in my mind and
write it forever on my heart so that it lives power-
fully in me every day.

God's Mercy on You Never Fails

Through the LORD's mercies
we are not consumed, because
His compassions fail not. They
are new every morning; great
is Your faithfulness.

LAMENTATIONS 3:22-23

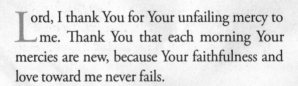

Lord, I thank You for Your unfailing mercy to me. Thank You that each morning Your mercies are new, because Your faithfulness and love toward me never fails.

Turn Your Heart to the Lord

Let us search out and examine our
ways, and turn back to the LORD.

LAMENTATIONS 3:40

Lord, I pray You would show me how I am. Help me to see what is truly in my heart and give me the strength to turn away from any sin and back to You.

God Will Give You a New Heart

I will give them one heart, and I will put a new spirit within them, and take the stony heart out of their flesh.

EZEKIEL 11:19

~

Lord, I ask that You would place a renewed heart within me. Take away any hardness in my mind, soul, and spirit that is not pleasing to You.

Keep God's Sabbath

I also gave them My Sabbaths, to
be a sign between them and Me,
that they might know that I am
the LORD who sanctifies them.

EZEKIEL 20:12

⤳

Lord, help me to keep Your Sabbaths holy and set apart to You as a time of rest and renewal, and a sacred sign that I am Your servant and You are my God.

Pray for All People

"As I live," says the Lord GOD,
"I have no pleasure in the death of
the wicked, but that the wicked
turn from his way and live."

EZEKIEL 33:11

❧

Lord, help me to remember to pray even for people I see as evil, because You desire that they repent of their wickedness and find salvation.

You Are a Living Temple for the Lord

*The Spirit lifted me up and brought
me into the inner court; and behold,
the glory of the LORD filled the temple.*

EZEKIEL 43:5

❧

Lord, I ask that You would lift me up into Your presence by the power of Your Spirit. Make me to be a pure and living temple, filled with Your glory.

Don't Let the World Determine Your Identity

Daniel purposed in his heart that he would not defile himself with the portion of the king's delicacies.

DANIEL 1:8

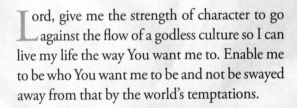

Lord, give me the strength of character to go against the flow of a godless culture so I can live my life the way You want me to. Enable me to be who You want me to be and not be swayed away from that by the world's temptations.

Stand for What
You Know Is Right

Let it be known to you, O king,
that we do not serve your gods,
nor will we worship the gold
image which you have set up.

DANIEL 3:18

Lord, I pray You will give me the faith and strength to resist the idols that clamor for my attention in this world. Help me to reject anything that is not of You so that I can worship only You.

Pray for Godly Leaders

The Most High God rules in the
kingdom of men, and appoints
over it whomever He chooses.

DANIEL 5:21

Lord, You rule over all things and You can lift up or tear down. I pray that You would raise up godly leaders in my country and bring down those who do evil. Deliver us from those who side with the enemy.

Ask God to Know Him Better

My people are destroyed for lack
of knowledge. Because you have
rejected knowledge, I also will reject
you from being priest for Me.

HOSEA 4:6

∽

Lord, I ask that You will fill me with an ever
greater understanding of You so that I never
act in ignorance of You and Your ways.

Refuse to Have Hardness of Heart

Break up your fallow ground, for it is time to seek the LORD, till He comes and rains righteousness on you.

HOSEA 10:12

Lord, show me any place where my heart has grown hard toward Your ways. Help me to plow up the crusty soil of my soul and prepare it for Your refreshing rain of restoration.

Repent Quickly Before God

*O Israel, return to the L*ORD *your*
God, for you have stumbled because
of your iniquity; take words with
*you, and return to the L*ORD*.*

HOSEA 14:1-2

⌒

Lord, help me to always quickly recognize
when I have disobeyed Your laws in any way
so that I can return fully to You with a repentant
heart and words of confession.

Don't Neglect to Fast and Pray

"Now, therefore," says the LORD, "turn to Me with all your heart, with fasting, with weeping, and with mourning."

JOEL 2:12

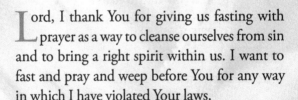

Lord, I thank You for giving us fasting with prayer as a way to cleanse ourselves from sin and to bring a right spirit within us. I want to fast and pray and weep before You for any way in which I have violated Your laws.

God Will Bring
Restoration to You

*"I will restore to you the years that
the swarming locust has eaten."*

JOEL 2:25

~

Lord, I thank You for Your love, grace, and compassion, which You show to all who turn to You. I praise You as the God of restoration and ask You to bring restoration where there has been great loss in my life.

God Will Save You
When You Call on Him

It shall come to pass that
whoever calls on the name of
the LORD shall be saved.

JOEL 2:32

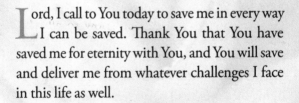

Lord, I call to You today to save me in every way
I can be saved. Thank You that You have
saved me for eternity with You, and You will save
and deliver me from whatever challenges I face
in this life as well.

Remember Who God Is

*He who forms mountains, and
creates the wind, who declares to
man what his thought is, and makes
the morning darkness, who treads
the high places of the earth—the
Lord God of hosts is His name.*

Amos 4:13

❧

Lord, You are the almighty Creator of the universe, and I praise and worship You alone.
You are in charge of my thoughts and in control
of my life, and I will never serve another.

Strive to Do What Is Right

Seek good and not evil, that
you may live; so the LORD God
of hosts will be with you.

Amos 5:14

Lord, help me to always be able to discern what is good and right from what is wrong and evil. I don't ever want to lose the fullness of Your presence in my life because I have made an allowance for sin.

Hunger for God to Speak into Your Life

I will send a famine on the land, not a famine of bread, nor a thirst for water, but of hearing the words of the LORD.

AMOS 8:11

Lord, I never want to experience the absence of Your powerful presence in my life. I want to always be able to hear Your voice speaking to my heart. Help me to never neglect Your Word or Your ways.

Refuse a Prideful Heart

*The pride of your heart
has deceived you.*

OBADIAH 3

Lord, I pray that You will deliver me from pride and the deception that comes along with it. I don't want to live my life in order to impress others but only to please You. Reveal to me all of the pride in my heart so that I can confess it to You as sin and be delivered from it.

Pray for the Heart of Your Nation

The day of the LORD upon all the nations is near; as you have done, it shall be done to you.

OBADIAH 15

Lord, I pray that You would pour out Your Spirit upon our nation. Raise up godly leaders who will do what's right so that we will not reap the terrible consequences of our collective sins.

Don't Run from God

*The men knew that he fled from
the presence of the LORD.*

JONAH 1:10

⁓

Lord, help me to never run away from You and
Your will in my life. When I become afraid
or just want my own way rather than Yours, I
pray that Your Spirit will convict me and help
me to choose obedience instead.

Forsake All Idols
and Find Mercy

Those who regard worthless
idols forsake their own Mercy.
But I will sacrifice to You with
the voice of thanksgiving.

JONAH 2:8-9

❧

Lord, help me to lay down any idols in my life so that I can continue to enjoy Your mercy in my life. I never want to idolize any thing or any person above my worship of You.

God Will Give You Another Chance

*The word of the LORD came
to Jonah the second time.*

JONAH 3:1

Lord, I praise You that You are the God of second chances. Thank You for Your mercy toward me when I fail and the gift of a new opportunity to please and serve You. Help me to come to You and not run from You when I don't do the right thing.

Turn to God and Away from Evil

God saw their works, that they turned from their evil way; and God relented from the disaster that He had said He would bring upon them, and He did not do it.

JONAH 3:10

❧

Lord, I turn to You and repent of any evil I have harbored in my thoughts or my life. Save me from the deserved consequences of my own sins.

Don't Compromise the Effectiveness of Your Prayers

They will cry to the LORD, but
He will not hear them; He will
even hide His face from them
at that time, because they have
been evil in their deeds.

MICAH 3:4

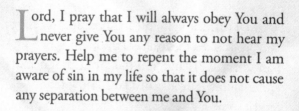

Lord, I pray that I will always obey You and never give You any reason to not hear my prayers. Help me to repent the moment I am aware of sin in my life so that it does not cause any separation between me and You.

God Always Fulfills His Prophecies

You, Bethlehem Ephrathah, though you are little among the thousands of Judah, yet out of you shall come forth to Me the One to be Ruler in Israel, whose goings forth are from of old, from everlasting.

MICAH 5:2

L ord, I thank You for the fulfillment of all Your prophecies, especially of the coming of Your Son to earth. Thank You that Your prophecies are unfailing. Because of that I know Jesus will return someday.

When You Fall, God Can Lift You Up

Do not rejoice over me, my enemy; when I fall, I will arise; when I sit in darkness, the LORD will be a light to me.

MICAH 7:8

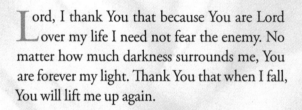

Lord, I thank You that because You are Lord over my life I need not fear the enemy. No matter how much darkness surrounds me, You are forever my light. Thank You that when I fall, You will lift me up again.

All People Are Accountable to God

*The LORD is slow to anger and
great in power, and will not
at all acquit the wicked.*

NAHUM 1:3

Lord, I thank You that You are patient and merciful to me, and to everyone who loves You, but You will not tolerate those who persist in their pursuit of evil.

God Is Your Strength in Troubled Times

The LORD is good, a stronghold in the day of trouble; and He knows those who trust in Him.

NAHUM 1:7

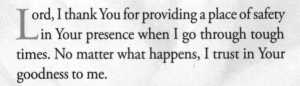

Lord, I thank You for providing a place of safety in Your presence when I go through tough times. No matter what happens, I trust in Your goodness to me.

Tell the Good News of God's Peace

Behold, on the mountains the feet of him who brings good tidings, who proclaims peace!

NAHUM 1:15

❧

Lord, I pray You would enable me to be a powerful messenger who brings good news of Your salvation and peace to others. I pray that I will always be a living witness to Your goodness through my actions and words.

Learn to Live by Faith

The just shall live by his faith.
HABAKKUK 2:4

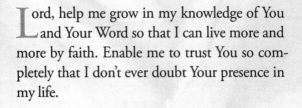

Lord, help me grow in my knowledge of You and Your Word so that I can live more and more by faith. Enable me to trust You so completely that I don't ever doubt Your presence in my life.

Reverence God at All Times

*The LORD is in His holy temple. Let
all the earth keep silence before Him.*

HABAKKUK 2:20

Lord, I bow my heart before You and praise
You for Your holiness. I worship You as the
God of all creation and Lord of all the earth. I
quiet my heart before You in awe of all that You
are.

God Is Your Source of Strength

The Lord God is my strength;
He will make my feet like
deer's feet, and He will make
me walk on my high hills.

HABAKKUK 3:19

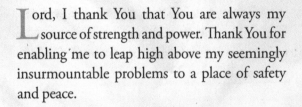

Lord, I thank You that You are always my source of strength and power. Thank You for enabling me to leap high above my seemingly insurmountable problems to a place of safety and peace.

Wait Quietly on the Lord

*Be silent in the presence of
the LORD God; for the day
of the LORD is at hand.*

ZEPHANIAH 1:7

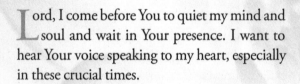

Lord, I come before You to quiet my mind and soul and wait in Your presence. I want to hear Your voice speaking to my heart, especially in these crucial times.

Seek the Lord Daily

Seek the LORD, all you meek of the earth, who have upheld His justice. Seek righteousness, seek humility.

ZEPHANIAH 2:3

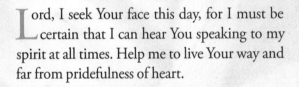

Lord, I seek Your face this day, for I must be certain that I can hear You speaking to my spirit at all times. Help me to live Your way and far from pridefulness of heart.

God Will Restore You

At that time I will bring you back,
even at the time I gather you.

ZEPHANIAH 3:20

◦∾◦

Lord, I thank You that You will restore me to right relationship with You whenever I have strayed from the path You have for me. Thank You that You will always bring me back when I turn to You in confession and repentance.

God's Spirit Is with You

*"My Spirit remains among you;
do not fear!" For thus says the
LORD of hosts: "Once more (it is a
little while) I will shake heaven
and earth, the sea and dry land;
and I will shake all nations."*

HAGGAI 2:5-7

Lord, how grateful I am that even in the midst
of the shaking that is going on in every
nation, in the sea and on land and in all the earth
that I can see, that Your Spirit stays among us
who love You and believe in You.

Sing Praise to God

*"Sing and rejoice, O daughter
of Zion! For behold, I am
coming and I will dwell in
your midst," says the LORD.*

ZECHARIAH 2:10

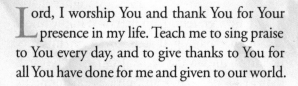

Lord, I worship You and thank You for Your
presence in my life. Teach me to sing praise
to You every day, and to give thanks to You for
all You have done for me and given to our world.

Live by the Power of God's Spirit

"Not by might nor by power, but by
My Spirit," says the LORD *of hosts.*

ZECHARIAH 4:6

Lord, help me to not strive to accomplish things in my own strength or power, but rather to turn to You, depending on Your Holy Spirit to strengthen and empower me to do what I need to do.

Live in Love and Truth

"Let none of you think evil in your heart against your neighbor; and do not love a false oath. For all these are things that I hate," says the LORD.

ZECHARIAH 8:17

Lord, help me to be filled with Your love so that I will always be a blessing to those around me. Teach me to live in truth so that I can speak in ways that please You.

Never Give Up Hope

Return to the stronghold, you
prisoners of hope. Even
today I declare that I will
restore double to you.

ZECHARIAH 9:12

Lord, help me to never doubt the hope You have put within me. Even when I suffer loss, thank You that You will restore more to me than I can imagine.

Ask God to Bless You

*Ask the LORD for rain in the
time of the latter rain.*

ZECHARIAH 10:1

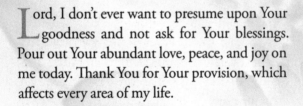

Lord, I don't ever want to presume upon Your goodness and not ask for Your blessings. Pour out Your abundant love, peace, and joy on me today. Thank You for Your provision, which affects every area of my life.

Love Your Brothers and Sisters in the Lord

Have we not all one Father? Has not one God created us? Why do we deal treacherously with one another?

MALACHI 2:10

Lord, I pray for all those who believe in You, that we would be in unity and not divided. I pray that we will acknowledge You as our heavenly Father and our Creator, and that we are brothers and sisters in the Lord, deserving of mutual love and respect toward one another.

Resist Even the
Thought of Divorce

*The LORD God of Israel says
that He hates divorce.*

MALACHI 2:16

❧

Lord, I know how You abhor the breaking of a
covenant with You—especially the covenant
of marriage, which is holy before You. Help me
to resist any thought of divorce. Keep me from
breaking any vow I make before You in any way.

Give Back to God

"Bring all the tithes into the storehouse, that there may be food in My house, and try Me now in this," says the LORD of hosts, "if I will not open for you the windows of heaven and pour out for you such blessing that there will not be room enough to receive it."

MALACHI 3:10

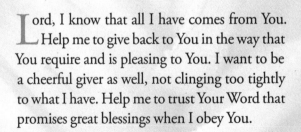

Lord, I know that all I have comes from You. Help me to give back to You in the way that You require and is pleasing to You. I want to be a cheerful giver as well, not clinging too tightly to what I have. Help me to trust Your Word that promises great blessings when I obey You.

Look to God First

Seek first the kingdom of God and
His righteousness, and all these
things shall be added to you.

MATTHEW 6:33

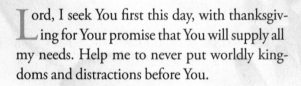

Lord, I seek You first this day, with thanksgiving for Your promise that You will supply all my needs. Help me to never put worldly kingdoms and distractions before You.

Speak Words That Build Up

I say to you that for every idle word men may speak, they will give account of it in the day of judgment. For by your words you will be justified, and by your words you will be condemned.

MATTHEW 12:36-37

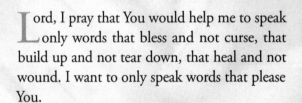

Lord, I pray that You would help me to speak only words that bless and not curse, that build up and not tear down, that heal and not wound. I want to only speak words that please You.

Find Someone to Pray With

*I say to you that if two of you agree
on earth concerning anything
that they ask, it will be done for
them by My Father in heaven.*

MATTHEW 18:19

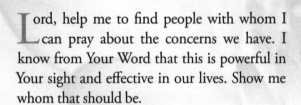

Lord, help me to find people with whom I can pray about the concerns we have. I know from Your Word that this is powerful in Your sight and effective in our lives. Show me whom that should be.

Believe God Will Answer Your Prayers

I say to you, whatever things you ask when you pray, believe that you receive them, and you will have them.

MARK 11:24

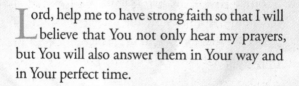

Lord, help me to have strong faith so that I will believe that You not only hear my prayers, but You will also answer them in Your way and in Your perfect time.

Pray to Resist Temptation

Watch and pray, lest you enter into temptation. The spirit indeed is willing, but the flesh is weak.

MARK 14:38

❧

Lord, I pray You would help me to always resist temptation. Enable me to recognize it well before it presents itself to me. Teach my spirit to rule over my flesh.

Ask God for a Good Heart

*A good man out of the good treasure
of his heart brings forth good;
and an evil man out of the evil
treasure of his heart brings forth
evil. For out of the abundance
of the heart his mouth speaks.*

LUKE 6:45

❧

Lord, I pray that You would pour into my heart Your love, joy, and goodness so that what overflows from my heart through the words I speak is pleasing to You.

You Have Authority over the Enemy

*Behold, I give you the authority
to trample on serpents and
scorpions, and over all the power
of the enemy, and nothing shall
by any means hurt you.*

LUKE 10:19

❧

Lord, I thank You that You have given me power over the enemy of my soul and my life, and therefore I am not subject to him, but I have authority over him. Give me strength to always resist the attempts of the enemy to thwart Your plans for my life.

Keep Praying and Don't Stop

*I say to you, ask, and it will be
given to you; seek, and you will find;
knock, and it will be opened to you.*

LUKE 11:9

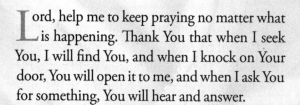

Lord, help me to keep praying no matter what
is happening. Thank You that when I seek
You, I will find You, and when I knock on Your
door, You will open it to me, and when I ask You
for something, You will hear and answer.

Nothing Is Impossible with God

*He said, "The things which
are impossible with men
are possible with God."*

LUKE 18:27

❧

Lord, I praise You as the all-powerful, almighty God of the universe, for whom nothing is impossible. The difficult situations I face in my own life are never too much for You to handle.

Jesus Is God's Greatest Gift to You

God so loved the world that He
gave His only begotten Son, that
whoever believes in Him should
not perish but have everlasting life.

JOHN 3:16

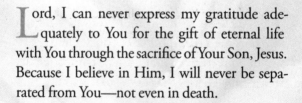

Lord, I can never express my gratitude adequately to You for the gift of eternal life with You through the sacrifice of Your Son, Jesus. Because I believe in Him, I will never be separated from You—not even in death.

Find Freedom in God's Word

*If you abide in My word, you
are My disciples indeed. And
you shall know the truth, and
the truth shall make you free.*

JOHN 8:31-32

~

Lord, help me to live in Your Word so that I can
become a true disciple of Yours. Help me to
live in Your truth so that I can be completely set
free from all lies of the enemy to my soul.

Stay Connected to the Vine

*I am the vine, you are the
branches. He who abides in Me,
and I in him, bears much fruit.*

JOHN 15:5

Lord, help me to always walk closely to You. I
am a small branch connected to You, Jesus,
as the true vine. Enable me to bear abundant
fruit all the days of my life.

Love Others

This is My commandment, that you love one another as I have loved you.

JOHN 15:12

∼∾

Lord, teach me how to love other people the way that You love them. Help me to lay down my life by sacrificing my time, effort, and material possessions—the substance of my life— to touch others with the love You have put in my heart.

Let the Holy Spirit Guide You

*When He, the Spirit of
truth, has come, He will
guide you into all truth.*

JOHN 16:13

❧

Lord, I thank You for Your Spirit of truth living in me and guiding me to live my life based on Your Word. Show me, Holy Spirit, how I should think in every situation. Enable me to always immediately discern a lie when it is presented to me.

Move in the Power of the Holy Spirit

You shall receive power when the Holy Spirit has come upon you; and you shall be witnesses to Me in Jerusalem, and in all Judea and Samaria, and to the end of the earth.

ACTS 1:8

❧

Lord, I pray that by the power of Your Holy Spirit You would enable me to do what You have called me to do. Help me to be a testimony of Your greatness to everyone You bring into my life, everywhere You send me.

Good Things Happen in the Midst of Difficulties

*We also glory in tribulations,
knowing that tribulation produces
perseverance; and perseverance,
character; and character, hope.*

Romans 5:3-4

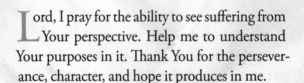

Lord, I pray for the ability to see suffering from Your perspective. Help me to understand Your purposes in it. Thank You for the perseverance, character, and hope it produces in me.

Nothing Can Separate
You from God's Love

Neither death nor life, nor angels
nor principalities nor powers, nor
things present nor things to come,
nor height nor depth, nor any
other created thing, shall be able
to separate us from the love of God
which is in Christ Jesus our Lord.

ROMANS 8:38-39

Lord, I thank You that nothing in this world can ever separate me from Your love—not anyone or anything, not the past or the future, and not even death. Thank You for Your unfailing and everlasting love for me.

Be Renewed in Your Mind

Do not be conformed to this world, but be transformed by the renewing of your mind, that you may prove what is that good and acceptable and perfect will of God.

ROMANS 12:2

Lord, I thank You that as I refuse to allow the world to mold me into *its* image, You are transforming my life by renewing my mind and perfecting me into *Your* image. Help me to surrender to the process so I can live out Your perfect will.

Treat Your Body as
if It Belongs to God

*You were bought at a price; therefore
glorify God in your body and in
your spirit, which are God's.*

1 CORINTHIANS 6:20

❧

Lord, help me to care for my body, always remembering I belong to You—body, soul, and spirit. I want to bring You glory in all I do, especially as I keep my physical body as the temple of Your Spirit.

Watch Out That You Don't Fall

Let him who thinks he stands
take heed lest he fall.

1 Corinthians 10:12

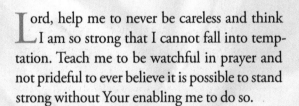

Lord, help me to never be careless and think I am so strong that I cannot fall into temptation. Teach me to be watchful in prayer and not prideful to ever believe it is possible to stand strong without Your enabling me to do so.

Whatever You Do,
Do It with Love

*Though I bestow all my goods to
feed the poor, and though I give
my body to be burned, but have
not love, it profits me nothing.*

1 CORINTHIANS 13:3

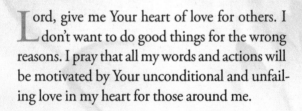

Lord, give me Your heart of love for others. I
don't want to do good things for the wrong
reasons. I pray that all my words and actions will
be motivated by Your unconditional and unfailing love in my heart for those around me.

Find Liberty
in God's Presence

The Lord is the Spirit; and where the
Spirit of the Lord is, there is liberty.

2 Corinthians 3:17

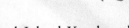

Lord, I thank You that wherever Your Spirit is I can find liberty. Thank You that Your Spirit in me is setting me free to daily be who You want me to be.

Become More Like the Lord

*We all, with unveiled face, beholding
as in a mirror the glory of the
Lord, are being transformed into
the same image from glory to glory,
just as by the Spirit of the Lord.*

2 CORINTHIANS 3:18

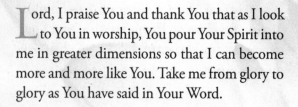

Lord, I praise You and thank You that as I look
to You in worship, You pour Your Spirit into
me in greater dimensions so that I can become
more and more like You. Take me from glory to
glory as You have said in Your Word.

Trust God's Grace to Sustain You

My grace is sufficient for you, for My strength is made perfect in weakness.

2 Corinthians 12:9

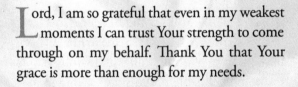

Lord, I am so grateful that even in my weakest moments I can trust Your strength to come through on my behalf. Thank You that Your grace is more than enough for my needs.

Stand Firm in the Freedom Jesus Has Given You

Stand fast therefore in the liberty by which Christ has made us free, and do not be entangled again with a yoke of bondage.

GALATIANS 5:1

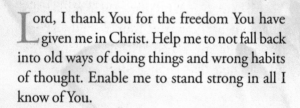

Lord, I thank You for the freedom You have given me in Christ. Help me to not fall back into old ways of doing things and wrong habits of thought. Enable me to stand strong in all I know of You.

Learn to Walk in the Spirit

If we live in the Spirit, let us
also walk in the Spirit.

GALATIANS 5:25

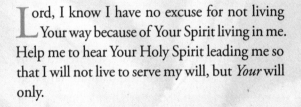

Lord, I know I have no excuse for not living Your way because of Your Spirit living in me. Help me to hear Your Holy Spirit leading me so that I will not live to serve my will, but *Your* will only.

Don't Grow Tired of Doing Right

Let us not grow weary
while doing good,
for in due season we shall reap
if we do not lose heart.

GALATIANS 6:9

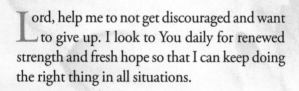

Lord, help me to not get discouraged and want to give up. I look to You daily for renewed strength and fresh hope so that I can keep doing the right thing in all situations.

Don't Carry Anger
in Your Heart

*"Be angry, and do not sin": do
not let the sun go down on your
wrath, nor give place to the devil.*

EPHESIANS 4:26-27

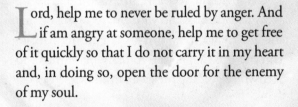

Lord, help me to never be ruled by anger. And
if am angry at someone, help me to get free
of it quickly so that I do not carry it in my heart
and, in doing so, open the door for the enemy
of my soul.

Walk Cautiously Each Day

See then that you walk circumspectly,
not as fools but as wise, redeeming
the time, because the days are evil.

EPHESIANS 5:15

Lord, help me to move through my life with great caution and wisdom, recognizing that the enemy wants to put a snare in my path to trip me up. Enable me to daily be sensitive to Your voice guiding me away from evil.

Don't Forget Your Spiritual Armor

*Take the helmet of salvation, and
the sword of the Spirit, which is
the word of God; praying always
with all prayer and supplication
in the Spirit, being watchful to
this end with all perseverance and
supplication for all the saints.*

EPHESIANS 6:17-18

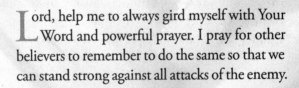

Lord, help me to always gird myself with Your
Word and powerful prayer. I pray for other
believers to remember to do the same so that we
can stand strong against all attacks of the enemy.

Be Aware of the Needs of People Around You

Let each of you look out not only for his own interests, but also for the interests of others.

<small>PHILIPPIANS 2:4</small>

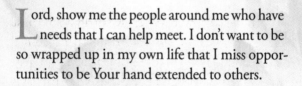

Lord, show me the people around me who have needs that I can help meet. I don't want to be so wrapped up in my own life that I miss opportunities to be Your hand extended to others.

Look Forward
and Not Behind

Forgetting those things which are behind and reaching forward to those things which are ahead, I press toward the goal for the prize of the upward call of God in Christ Jesus.

PHILIPPIANS 3:13-14

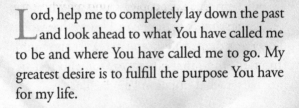

Lord, help me to completely lay down the past and look ahead to what You have called me to be and where You have called me to go. My greatest desire is to fulfill the purpose You have for my life.

Take All Your Concerns to God

Be anxious for nothing, but in everything by prayer and supplication, with thanksgiving, let your requests be made known to God.

PHILIPPIANS 4:6

⁓

Lord, help me to be anxiety-free by taking every concern to You in prayer. I know that when I do, Your peace will soothe my heart and mind. Teach me to be thankful to You for who You are, no matter what situation I am facing.

Commit to Pleasing the Lord

*Walk worthy of the Lord, fully
pleasing Him, being fruitful in
every good work and increasing
in the knowledge of God.*

COLOSSIANS 1:10

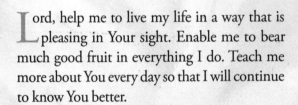

Lord, help me to live my life in a way that is
pleasing in Your sight. Enable me to bear
much good fruit in everything I do. Teach me
more about You every day so that I will continue
to know You better.

You Have Been Set Free from the Enemy

He has delivered us from the power of darkness and conveyed us into the kingdom of the Son of His love.

COLOSSIANS 1:13

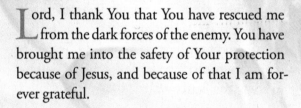

Lord, I thank You that You have rescued me from the dark forces of the enemy. You have brought me into the safety of Your protection because of Jesus, and because of that I am forever grateful.

Keep Looking Up to God

Set your mind on things above,
not on things on the earth.

COLOSSIANS 3:2

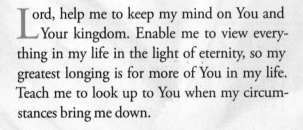

Lord, help me to keep my mind on You and Your kingdom. Enable me to view everything in my life in the light of eternity, so my greatest longing is for more of You in my life. Teach me to look up to You when my circumstances bring me down.

Be Thankful
in Every Situation

In everything give thanks;
for this is the will of God
in Christ Jesus for you.

1 THESSALONIANS 5:18

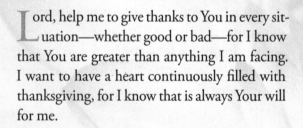

Lord, help me to give thanks to You in every situation—whether good or bad—for I know that You are greater than anything I am facing. I want to have a heart continuously filled with thanksgiving, for I know that is always Your will for me.

God Will Protect You from Evil

The Lord is faithful, who will establish you and guard you from the evil one.

2 THESSALONIANS 3:3

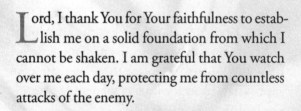

Lord, I thank You for Your faithfulness to establish me on a solid foundation from which I cannot be shaken. I am grateful that You watch over me each day, protecting me from countless attacks of the enemy.

Pray for Your Leaders

*I exhort first of all that supplications,
prayers, intercessions, and giving of
thanks be made for all men, for kings
and all who are in authority, that
we may lead a quiet and peaceable
life in all godliness and reverence.*

1 TIMOTHY 2:1-2

Lord, I pray for all the leaders in our nation that they will be righteous and honest. Raise up godly leaders to replace those who are corrupt. Thank You for leaders who are wise and not foolish.

Lift Your Hands
to God in Prayer

*I desire therefore that the men pray
everywhere, lifting up holy hands,
without wrath and doubting.*

1 TIMOTHY 2:8

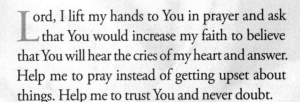

Lord, I lift my hands to You in prayer and ask
that You would increase my faith to believe
that You will hear the cries of my heart and answer.
Help me to pray instead of getting upset about
things. Help me to trust You and never doubt.

Don't Be Led Astray by Deception

The Spirit expressly says that in latter times some will depart from the faith, giving heed to deceiving spirits and doctrines of demons.

1 Timothy 4:1

~⁂~

Lord, keep me undeceived so that I never depart from the faith in even the smallest way. Give me discernment so that I can easily recognize the doctrine of evil people—who are themselves deceived—and reject their teaching.

Find Peace in Godly Living

Godliness with contentment
is great gain.
1 Timothy 6:6

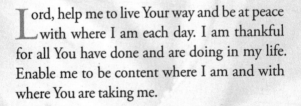

Lord, help me to live Your way and be at peace with where I am each day. I am thankful for all You have done and are doing in my life. Enable me to be content where I am and with where You are taking me.

Love God and Not Money

The love of money is a root of all kinds of evil, for which some have strayed from the faith in their greediness, and pierced themselves through with many sorrows.

1 TIMOTHY 6:10

❧

Lord, help me to never allow a quest for money to lead me away from You and Your laws. Keep me from becoming greedy and reaping the sorrows that come along with it.

God Gives You
Power and Not Fear

*God has not given us a spirit
of fear, but of power and of
love and of a sound mind.*

2 TIMOTHY 1:7

Lord, I thank You that I don't need to live in fear, because You have given me Your power and Your love, and a sound mind that can discern the difference.

Play According to the Rules

If anyone competes in athletics,
he is not crowned unless he
competes according to the rules.

2 Timothy 2:5

Lord, I pray that I will be able to run the race of life according to Your rules so that I can receive the crown of life You have for those who love and serve You.

Strive to Understand God's Word

*Be diligent to present yourself
approved to God, a worker who
does not need to be ashamed, rightly
dividing the word of truth.*

2 TIMOTHY 2:15

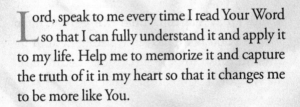

Lord, speak to me every time I read Your Word so that I can fully understand it and apply it to my life. Help me to memorize it and capture the truth of it in my heart so that it changes me to be more like You.

Finish the Race Well

I have fought the good fight, I have
finished the race, I have kept the
faith. Finally, there is laid up for
me the crown of righteousness,
which the Lord, the righteous
Judge, will give to me on that Day.

2 Timothy 4:7-8

❧

Lord, I pray that You would enable me to fight
the good fight and stand strong in faith in
order to finish my life successfully and receive
the symbol of righteousness that You have wait-
ing for me.

You Are Destined for Heaven

The Lord will deliver me from
every evil work and preserve me
for His heavenly kingdom.

2 TIMOTHY 4:18

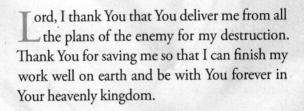

Lord, I thank You that You deliver me from all the plans of the enemy for my destruction. Thank You for saving me so that I can finish my work well on earth and be with You forever in Your heavenly kingdom.

Live a Godly Life

The grace of God that brings
salvation has appeared to all
men, teaching us that, denying
ungodliness and worldly lusts, we
should live soberly, righteously,
and godly in the present age.

Titus 2:11-12

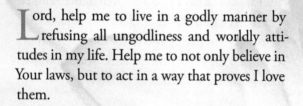

Lord, help me to live in a godly manner by refusing all ungodliness and worldly attitudes in my life. Help me to not only believe in Your laws, but to act in a way that proves I love them.

Pray for Other Believers

I thank my God, making mention
of you always in my prayers,
hearing of your love and faith
which you have toward the Lord
Jesus and toward all the saints.

PHILEMON 1:4-5

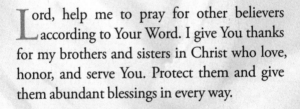

Lord, help me to pray for other believers according to Your Word. I give You thanks for my brothers and sisters in Christ who love, honor, and serve You. Protect them and give them abundant blessings in every way.

Come to God Without Hesitation

Let us therefore come boldly
to the throne of grace, that we
may obtain mercy and find
grace to help in time of need.

HEBREWS 4:16

❧

Lord, I come before You without any reservation, thankful for Your grace without judgment, and Your undeserved mercy. Enable me to show that same mercy and grace to others in need as You have shown to me.

Have Faith for
What You Don't Yet See

*Faith is the substance of things hoped
for, the evidence of things not seen.*

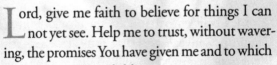

Lord, give me faith to believe for things I can
not yet see. Help me to trust, without waver-
ing, the promises You have given me and to which
I lay claim as Your child.

God Rewards You
When You Seek Him

*Without faith it is impossible to
please Him, for he who comes
to God must believe that He
is, and that He is a rewarder of
those who diligently seek Him.*

HEBREWS 11:6

⁓

Lord, I believe that You are the almighty God
of the universe and that You care about my
life. I pray that my faith will grow strong and be
pleasing to You. I seek to know You more, and I
thank You for Your many rewards for loving You
and living Your way.

Let Nothing Hinder Your Walk with God

Let us lay aside every weight, and the sin which so easily ensnares us, and let us run with endurance the race that is set before us.

Hebrews 12:1

Lord, help me to cast away anything that hinders or slows my walk with You so that I can run the race set before me with great strength and endurance. Enable me to avoid any snare of sin and to overcome all burdens and challenges by the power of Your Spirit.

God Will Not Leave You

Let your conduct be without covetousness; be content with such things as you have. For He Himself has said, "I will never leave you nor forsake you."

HEBREWS 13:5

❧

Lord, I confess as sin anytime I have looked at what someone else has and have wanted it. Help me to always be content with what You have given me. Thank You that I don't have to be afraid of lack, because You have promised to never forsake me.

Give Thanks in Troubled Times

*Count it all joy when you fall
into various trials, knowing that
the testing of your faith produces
patience. But let patience have its
perfect work, that you may be perfect
and complete, lacking nothing.*

JAMES 1:2-4

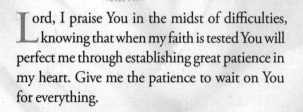

Lord, I praise You in the midst of difficulties,
knowing that when my faith is tested You will
perfect me through establishing great patience in
my heart. Give me the patience to wait on You
for everything.

Stand Strong Against Temptation

Blessed is the man who endures temptation; for when he has been approved, he will receive the crown of life which the Lord has promised to those who love Him.

JAMES 1:12

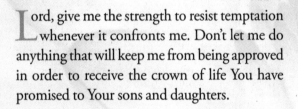

Lord, give me the strength to resist temptation whenever it confronts me. Don't let me do anything that will keep me from being approved in order to receive the crown of life You have promised to Your sons and daughters.

Be a Doer of the Word

*He who looks into the perfect
law of liberty and continues in
it, and is not a forgetful hearer
but a doer of the work, this one
will be blessed in what he does.*

JAMES 1:25

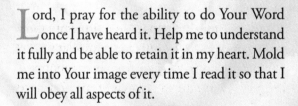

Lord, I pray for the ability to do Your Word
once I have heard it. Help me to understand
it fully and be able to retain it in my heart. Mold
me into Your image every time I read it so that I
will obey all aspects of it.

Watch What You Say

*No man can tame the tongue. It is
an unruly evil, full of deadly poison.*

JAMES 3:8

❧

Lord, I pray that Your Spirit would help me to control what I say so that every word from my mouth will only bless others and glorify You. Keep me from ever speaking deadly words that destroy.

Humble Yourself
Before God

Humble yourselves in the sight of
the Lord, and He will lift you up.

JAMES 4:10

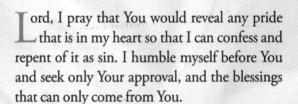

Lord, I pray that You would reveal any pride that is in my heart so that I can confess and repent of it as sin. I humble myself before You and seek only Your approval, and the blessings that can only come from You.

Remember Who You Are

*You are a chosen generation, a
royal priesthood, a holy nation,
His own special people, that you
may proclaim the praises of Him
who called you out of darkness
into His marvelous light.*

1 PETER 2:9

Lord, I thank You that I am a child of Yours
and You have chosen me as part of Your special people who are called out of darkness into
Your light to proclaim praise to You. Help me to
never forget that for even a moment.

Share Your Hope
with Others

Sanctify the Lord God in your hearts, and always be ready to give a defense to everyone who asks you a reason for the hope that is in you, with meekness and fear.

1 PETER 3:15

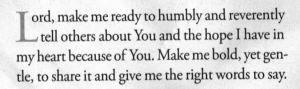

Lord, make me ready to humbly and reverently tell others about You and the hope I have in my heart because of You. Make me bold, yet gentle, to share it and give me the right words to say.

Watch Out for the Enemy

Be sober, be vigilant; because
your adversary the devil walks
about like a roaring lion, seeking
whom he may devour.

1 PETER 5:8

Lord, I pray that You will give me great discernment so I can always be aware of the enemy's plans for my life. Hide me in Your shadow so that the adversary cannot even approach me as he seeks to do harm.

Don't Return to Practices from Which You Have Been Delivered

If, after they have escaped the pollutions of the world through the knowledge of the Lord and Savior Jesus Christ, they are again entangled in them and overcome, the latter end is worse for them than the beginning.

2 PETER 2:20

Lord, I know that if believers backslide from what they know is right in You, their life will be worse than before they knew You. Don't let that ever happen to me, I pray. Help me to be so strong in You that I am never lured back to my old sinful ways.

Be Always Awaiting the Return of Jesus

What manner of persons ought you to be in holy conduct and godliness, looking for and hastening the coming of the day of God, because of which the heavens will be dissolved, being on fire, and the elements will melt with fervent heat? Nevertheless we, according to His promise, look for new heavens and a new earth in which righteousness dwells.

2 Peter 3:11-13

❧

Lord, help me remember both the fleeting and transitory nature of this world and the certainty of life with You in eternity. How I long for the day when You return and Your righteousness reigns. I wait for You with hope in my heart.

Stay Cleansed from All Sin

If we confess our sins, He is faithful
and just to forgive us our sins and to
cleanse us from all unrighteousness.

1 JOHN 1:9

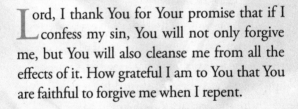

Lord, I thank You for Your promise that if I confess my sin, You will not only forgive me, but You will also cleanse me from all the effects of it. How grateful I am to You that You are faithful to forgive me when I repent.

Do Not Love the Things of the World

*Do not love the world or the things in
the world. If anyone loves the world,
the love of the Father is not in him.*

1 John 2:15

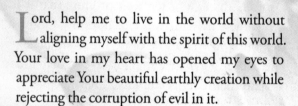

Lord, help me to live in the world without aligning myself with the spirit of this world. Your love in my heart has opened my eyes to appreciate Your beautiful earthly creation while rejecting the corruption of evil in it.

God's Love Evaporates
Your Fear

There is no fear in love; but perfect
love casts out fear, because fear
involves torment. But he who fears
has not been made perfect in love.

1 JOHN 4:18

⌘

Lord, I pray that Your perfect love in my life
and my heart will take away all fear from my
mind. I refuse the torment of ungodly fear and
embrace Your love, which casts it out.

Love God by Obeying Him

*This is love, that we walk according
to His commandments.*

2 John 6

෴

Lord, help me to show my love for You by obeying You in every way. Loving You makes me want to please You by living Your way, but sometimes I falter and I know I need Your power to enable me to do the right thing.

Don't Imitate Ungodly People

Do not imitate what is evil, but
what is good. He who does
good is of God, but he who
does evil has not seen God.

3 JOHN 11

Lord, help me not to pattern my life in any way after ungodly people. Enable me to recognize evil and refuse to emulate it in any way. I want to show that I have seen and know You by living Your way.

Reject Those Who Mock God

Remember the words which were
spoken before by the apostles of our
Lord Jesus Christ: how they told
you that there would be mockers
in the last time who would walk
according to their own ungodly lusts.
These are sensual persons, who cause
divisions, not having the Spirit.

JUDE 17-19

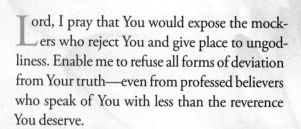

Lord, I pray that You would expose the mockers who reject You and give place to ungodliness. Enable me to refuse all forms of deviation from Your truth—even from professed believers who speak of You with less than the reverence You deserve.

Jesus Has the Keys to Death and Hell

I am He who lives, and was dead, and behold, I am alive forevermore. Amen. And I have the keys of Hades and of Death.

Revelation 1:18

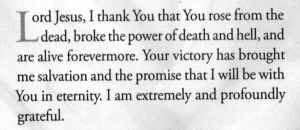

Lord Jesus, I thank You that You rose from the dead, broke the power of death and hell, and are alive forevermore. Your victory has brought me salvation and the promise that I will be with You in eternity. I am extremely and profoundly grateful.

Keep Your Love for God Alive

I have this against you, that you have left your first love.

REVELATION 2:4

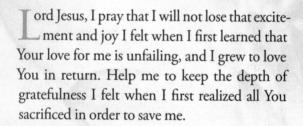

Lord Jesus, I pray that I will not lose that excitement and joy I felt when I first learned that Your love for me is unfailing, and I grew to love You in return. Help me to keep the depth of gratefulness I felt when I first realized all You sacrificed in order to save me.

Never Deny
the Name of Jesus

I have set before you an open door,
and no one can shut it; for you have
a little strength, have kept My word,
and have not denied My name.

REVELATION 3:8

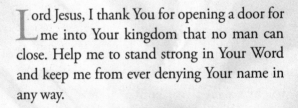

Lord Jesus, I thank You for opening a door for me into Your kingdom that no man can close. Help me to stand strong in Your Word and keep me from ever denying Your name in any way.

Keep the Door of Your Heart Open to Jesus

Behold, I stand at the door and knock. If anyone hears My voice and opens the door, I will come in to him and dine with him, and he with Me.

REVELATION 3:20

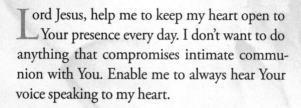

Lord Jesus, help me to keep my heart open to Your presence every day. I don't want to do anything that compromises intimate communion with You. Enable me to always hear Your voice speaking to my heart.

Keep Watching for the Lord's Return

Behold, I am coming as a thief.
Blessed is he who watches, and
keeps his garments, lest he walk
naked and they see his shame.

REVELATION 16:15

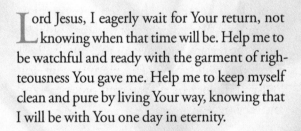

Lord Jesus, I eagerly wait for Your return, not knowing when that time will be. Help me to be watchful and ready with the garment of righteousness You gave me. Help me to keep myself clean and pure by living Your way, knowing that I will be with You one day in eternity.

Jesus Rewards Those Who Love Him

*Behold, I am coming quickly, and
My reward is with Me, to give to
every one according to his work.*

REVELATION 22:12

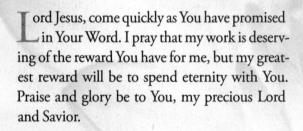

Lord Jesus, come quickly as You have promised in Your Word. I pray that my work is deserving of the reward You have for me, but my greatest reward will be to spend eternity with You. Praise and glory be to You, my precious Lord and Savior.

Other Books
by Stormie Omartian

The Power of a Praying® Life
Stormie Omartian has led millions to pray. Each of her books have opened up the mystery of prayer and helped readers approach God with confidence and experience His power. Stormie now shares what it means to connect deeply with God and find freedom, wholeness, and success in every circumstance.

The Power of a Praying® Wife Devotional
In 100 brand-new devotions, prayers, and supporting Scriptures, Stormie offers a praying wife fresh ways to pray for her husband, herself, and her marriage. These easy-to-read devotions will increase any wife's understanding, strength, and peace, and provide her with perspective on the situations and challenges she faces.

The Power of Prayer™ to Change Your Marriage
Stormie encourages husbands or wives to pray to protect their relationship from 14 serious threats that can lead to unsatisfying marriages or even divorce. Biblical, prayerful insights addressing communication breakdown, struggles with finances, anger, infidelity, parenting struggles, and more, will lead couples to healing and restoration.

THE POWER OF PRAYING® FOR YOUR ADULT CHILDREN
In this important follow-up to *The Power of a Praying® Parent*, Stormie shares stories from other parents and insight gleaned from personal experience to help parents pray with the power of God's Word over their adult children's relationships, future, integrity, faith, and trials.

THE POWER OF PRAYING® THROUGH THE BIBLE
In her first devotional, Stormie journeys from Genesis to Revelation and reveals how to communicate with God, embrace His promises, walk with Jesus, and listen to the Spirit's leading. This gathering from *The Power of a Praying® Woman Bible* inspires readers with the truths of God's Word and is the perfect complement to *Praying the Bible into Your Life*.

POWERFUL PRAYERS FOR TROUBLED TIMES
In this easy-to-carry pocket book, Stormie tackles genuine questions about praying for our country. She offers sample prayers you can use to pray for government and community leaders, the heroic men and women who protect us (police officers, firefighters, soldiers), and the welfare and healing of our nation.

THE POWER OF A PRAYING® WOMAN

Stormie's deep knowledge of Scripture and examples from her own life provide guidance for women who seek to trust God, maintain a right heart, and give their lives over to God's purpose.

THE POWER OF A PRAYING® WOMAN BIBLE

This devotional study Bible with NIV text contains brief introductions for each book of the Bible, inspiring and informative articles and sidebars, and all new prayers Stormie uses to apply verses to her prayer life.

To learn more about books by Stormie Omartian
or to read sample chapters, log on to our website:

www.harvesthousepublishers.com

HARVEST HOUSE PUBLISHERS

EUGENE, OREGON